Bugs in My Backyard

I See Fireflies

By Julia Jaske

I see a firefly.

I see a firefly swarm.

3

I see a firefly crawling.

I see a firefly glowing.

I see a firefly exploring.

I see a firefly waiting.

8 I see a firefly smelling.

I see a firefly drinking.

I see a firefly flying.

I see a firefly climbing.

I see a firefly flashing.

I see a firefly saying hello!

Word List

firefly

swarm

crawling

glowing

exploring

waiting

smelling

drinking

flying

climbing

flashing

saying

hello